Bedtime

HOUGHTON MIFFLIN   BOSTON

Amy is done with her bath.
It's time for bed.

"I'm not ONE BIT tired!"
says Amy.

"Go to bed early, and wake up early tomorrow," says her mother. "You'll have more time to make trouble!"

"That makes sense,"
says Amy.
Then her mother tucks her
in bed.